W9-ANT-856

TO:

Mark Choa

FROM:

Aunt Lina

Tender and tough. Faithfully firm.
Patiently urgent. Eagerly tolerant.
Softly shouting. Gentle. Thunder.

That's how John saw Jesus.
May you, too, experience
His gentle thunder.

A Gentle Thunder

MAX LUCADO

WORD PUBLISHING

Dallas·London·Vancouver·Melbourne

Copyright © 1996 by Max Lucado
All rights reserved. No portion of this
publication may be reproduced, stored in a
retrieval system, or transmitted in any form or by
any means—electronic, mechanical, photocopy,
recording, or any other—except for brief
quotations in printed reviews, without
the prior permission of the publisher.

Unless otherwise indicated, all Scripture
quotations are from the New Century Version
of the Bible, copyright ©1987, 1988, 1991,
Word Publishing.

ISBN 0-8499-5142-9

Printed in Hong Kong

1

HIS VOICE, OUR CHOICE

When you were in trouble,
you called, and I saved you.
I answered you with thunder.

Psalm 81:7

good pilot does what it takes to get his passengers home.

I saw a good example of this while flying somewhere over Missouri. The airline attendant told us to take our seats because of impending turbulence. It was a rowdy flight, and the folks weren't quick to respond; so she warned us again. "The flight is about to get bumpy. For your own safety, take your seats."

Most did. But a few didn't, so she

changed her tone, "Ladies and gentle-men, for your own good, take your seats."

I thought everyone was seated. But apparently I was wrong, for the next voice we heard was that of the pilot. "This is Captain Brown," he advised. "People have gotten hurt by going to the bathroom instead of staying in their seats. Let's be very clear about our responsibilities. My job is to get you through the storm. Your job is to do what I say. Now sit down and buckle up!"

About that time the bathroom door opened and a red-faced fellow with a sheepish grin exited and took his seat.

Was the pilot wrong in what he did? Was the pilot being insensitive or unthoughtful? No, just the opposite. He would rather the man be safe and embarrassed than uninformed and hurt.

Good pilots do what it takes to get their passengers home.

So does God. Here is the key question. How far do you want God to go in getting your attention? If God has to choose between your eternal safety and your earthly comfort, which do you hope he chooses? Don't answer too quickly. Give it some thought.

If God sees you standing when you should be sitting, if God sees you at risk rather than safe, how far do you want him to go in getting your attention?

What if he moved you to another land? (As he did Abraham.) What if he called you out of retirement? (Remember Moses?) How about the voice of an angel or the bowel of a fish?

(À la Gideon and Jonah.) How about a promotion like Daniel's or a demotion like Samson's?

God does what it takes to get our attention. Isn't that the message of the Bible? Isn't that *the* message of the Bible? The relentless pursuit of God. God on the hunt. God in the search. Peeking under the bed for hiding kids, stirring the bushes for lost sheep. Cupping hand to mouth and shouting into the canyon. Wrestling with us Jacobs in the muddy Jabboks of life.

For all its peculiarities and unevenness, the Bible has a simple story. God made man. Man rejected God. God won't give up until he wins him back. From Moses in Moab to John on Patmos, the voice can be heard: "I'm the pilot. You're the passenger. My job is to get you home. Your job is to do what I say."

God is as creative as he is relentless. The same hand that sent manna to Israel sent Uzzah to his death. The same hand that set the children free from Israel also sent them captive to

Babylon. Both kind and stern. Tender and tough. Faithfully firm. Patiently urgent. Eagerly tolerant. Softly shouting. Gently thundering.

Gentle thunder.

That's how John saw Jesus. John's Gospel has two themes: the voice of God and the choice of man. And since this book is based on John, you'll see the same tandem: His voice. Our choice.

Jesus said, "I am the bread that gives life. I am the light of the world. I am the resurrection and the life. I am

the light of the world. I am the door. I
am the way, the truth, and the life. I will
come back and take you with me."

Jesus proclaiming—ever offering
but never forcing:

Standing over the crippled man:
"Do you want to be well?" (John 5:6).

Eye to eye with the blind man, now
healed: "Do you believe in the Son of
Man?" (John 9:35).

Near the tomb of Lazarus, probing
the heart of Martha: "Everyone who
lives and believes in me will never die.

Martha, do you believe this?" (John 11:26).

Testing Pilate's motive: "Is that your own question, or did others tell you about me?" (John 18:34).

The first time John hears Jesus speak, Jesus asks a question, "What are you looking for?" (John 1:38). Among Jesus' last words is yet another: "Do you love me?" (John 21:17).

This is the Jesus John remembers. The honest questions. The thundering claims. The gentle touch. Never going where not invited, but once invited never stopping until he's finished, until a choice has been made.

God will whisper. He will shout. He will touch and tug. He will take away our burdens; he'll even take away our blessings. If there are a thousand steps between us and him, he will take all but one. But he will leave the final one for us. The choice is ours.

Please understand. His goal is not to make you happy. His goal is to make you his. His goal is not to get you what you want; it is to get you what you need. And if that means a jolt or two to get you in your seat, then be jolted. Earthly discomfort is a glad swap for heavenly peace. Jesus said, "In this world you will have trouble, but be brave! I have defeated the world" (John 16:33).

How could he speak with such authority? What gave him the right to take command? Simple. He, like the pilot, knows what we don't, and he can see what we can't.

What did the pilot know? He knew

how to fly the plane.

What did the pilot see? Storm clouds ahead.

What does God know? He knows how to navigate history.

What does God see? I think you get the message.

God wants to get you home safely.

Just think of him as your pilot. Think of yourself as his passenger. Consider this book as in-flight reading— and think twice before you get up to go to the potty.

2

THE HOUND
OF HEAVEN

I saw the Spirit come down in the form of a dove and rest on him. Until then I did not know who the Christ was. But the God who sent me to baptize with water told me, "You will see the Spirit come down and rest on a man; he is the One who will baptize with the Holy Spirit." I have seen this happen, and I tell you the truth: This is the Son of God.

John 1:32–34

*J*ohn the Baptist saw a dove and believed. James Whittaker saw a sea gull and believed. Who's to say the one who sent the first didn't send the second?

James Whittaker was a member of the handpicked crew that flew the B-17 Flying Fortress captained by Eddie Rickenbacker. Anybody who remembers October of 1942 remembers the day Rickenbacker and his crew were reported lost at sea.

Somewhere over the Pacific, out of radio range, the plane ran out of fuel and crashed into the ocean. The nine men spent the next month floating in three rafts. They battled the heat, the storms, and the water. Sharks, some ten feet long, would ram their nine-foot boats. After only eight days their rations were eaten or destroyed by saltwater. It would take a miracle to survive.

One morning after their daily devotions, Rickenbacker leaned his head back against the raft and pulled

his hat over his eyes. A bird landed
on his head. He peered out from under
his hat. Every eye was on him. He
instinctively knew it was a sea gull.

Rickenbacker caught it, and the
crew ate it. The bird's intestines were
used for bait to catch fish . . . and
the crew survived to tell the story.
A story about a stranded crew with
no hope or help in sight. A story about
prayers offered and prayers answered.
A story about a visitor from an unknown land traveling a great distance

to give his life as a sacrifice.

A story of salvation.

A story much like our own. Weren't we, like the crew, stranded? Weren't we, like the crew, praying? And weren't we, like the crew, rescued by a visitor we've never seen through a sacrifice we'll never forget?

You may have heard the Rickenbacker story before. You may have even heard it from me. You may have read it in one of my books. Coreen Schweenk did. She was engaged to the only crew member who did not survive, young Sgt. Alex Kacymarcyck. As a result of a 1985 reunion of the crew, Mrs. Schweenk learned that the widow of James Whittaker lived only eighty miles from her house. The two women met and shared their stories.

After reading this story in my book *In the Eye of the Storm*, Mrs. Schweenk felt compelled to write to me. The real miracle, she informed me, was not a bird on the head of Eddie Rickenbacker but a change in the heart of James

Whittaker. The greatest event of that day was not the rescue of a crew but the rescue of a soul.

James Whittaker was an unbeliever. The plane crash didn't change his unbelief. The days facing death didn't cause him to reconsider his destiny. In fact, Mrs. Whittaker said her husband grew irritated with John Bartak, a crew member who continually read his Bible privately and aloud.

But his protests didn't stop Bartak from reading. Nor did Whittaker's resistance stop the Word from penetrating his soul. Unknown to Whittaker, the soil of his heart was being plowed. For it was one morning after a Bible reading that the sea gull landed on Captain Rickenbacker's head.

And at that moment Jim became a believer.

I chuckled when I read the letter. Not at the letter; I believe every word of it. Nor at James Whittaker. I have every reason to believe his conversion was real. But I had to chuckle at . . . please excuse me . . . I had to chuckle at God.

Isn't that just like him? Who would go to such extremes to save a soul? Such an effort to get a guy's attention. The rest of the world is occupied with Germany and Hitler. Every headline is reporting the actions of Roosevelt and Churchill. The globe is locked in a battle for freedom . . . and the Father is in the Pacific sending a missionary pigeon to save a soul. Oh, the lengths to which God will go to get our attention and win our affection.

The Hound of Heaven

In 1893 Francis Thompson, a Roman Catholic poet, described God as the "Hound of Heaven":

I fled Him, down the nights and down the days;
I fled Him, down the arches of the years;
I fled Him, down the labyrinthian ways
    Of my own mind;
    and in the mist of tears
I hid from Him, and under running laughter,
    Up vestaed hopes I sped
And shot precipitated
Adown Titanic glooms.[1]

Thompson speaks of Jesus as "that tremendous lover, pursuing me with his love." Jesus follows with "unhurrying chase and unperturbed pace, deliberate speed, majestic instancy." And in the end Jesus speaks, reminding us, "Alas, thou knowest not how little worthy of any love thou art. Whom wilt thou find to love ignoble thee, save me, save only me? For that which I took from thee I did but take, not for thy harm but that thou might seek it in my arms."[2]

Do you have room for such a

picture of God? Can you see God as the "tremendous lover, pursuing us with his love"? During the first week of Jesus' ministry he calls his first disciples. Why do they come? Who influences their choice? Note the verbs associated with Jesus in John 1.

> Jesus turned . . . v. 38
>
> Jesus asked . . . v. 38
>
> Jesus answered . . . v. 39
>
> Jesus looked . . . v. 42
>
> Jesus decided . . . v. 43
>
> Jesus found . . . v. 43

It's clear who does the work. If anyone is in Christ, it is because Christ has called him or her. Christ may use a sermon. He may inspire a conversation. He may speak through a song. But in every case Christ is the One who calls.

Consider these examples:

One evening, John Wesley entered a brief account in his journal. He wrote of going unwillingly to a meeting of a society in Aldersgate Street in London where one of the group was reading the preface to Luther's *Commentary on the*

Epistle to the Romans. Did you get the picture? He went unwillingly, a stranger to a small group, listening to a two-hundred-year-old piece of literature. And yet he wrote, "About a quarter before nine I felt my heart strangely warmed."[3]

In his classic work *Confessions,* Augustine tells of the turning point in his life. Torn between the temptation of a mistress and the quiet call of the Spirit of God, he was sitting on a bench under a fig tree, his Bible open, his

eyesight fogged by tears. He heard a
voice calling from a neighboring house,
"Pick it up . . . Pick it up . . ."

The voice was not addressed to
Augustine; no doubt children were
calling to one another in a game. However, the voice stirred Augustine in his
solitude, and he did what the voice
commanded. He picked up his Bible
and read it. The passage before him was
Romans 13:13–14: "Let us live in a
right way, like people who belong to the
day. We should not have wild parties or

get drunk. There should be no sexual sins of any kind, no fighting or jealousy. But clothe yourselves with the Lord Jesus Christ and forget about satisfying your sinful self."

He heard the voice of God, bade farewell to his mistress, and followed Christ.[4]

Novelist Frederick Buechner was twenty-seven years old and living alone in New York City, trying to write a book when he, a non-churchgoer, went to church. On impulse. The preacher spoke on the topic of crowning Christ in your heart. Jesus refused the crown of Satan in the wilderness but accepts the crown of his people when we confess him. The preacher went on for quite some time with words that sounded nice but didn't stick.

But then he said something that Buechner never forgot. I'll let him tell you:

*And then with his head bobbing
up and down so that his glasses*

*tittered, he said in his odd sandy
voice, the voice of an old nurse, that
the coronation of Jesus took place
among confession and tears and, as
God is my witness, great laughter,
he said. Jesus is crowned among
confession and tears and great
laughter, and at that phrase great
laughter, for reasons I have never
satisfactorily understood, the great
wall of China crumbled and
Atlantis rose up out of the sea, and
on Madison Avenue, at 73rd Street,*

tears leapt from my eyes as though
I had been struck in the face.[5]

Too bizarre? Think for a moment about your world. Remember that voice, that face, that event? Wasn't there a time when the common bush of the wilderness was ablaze with a voice that left you stuttering? For Wesley it was a reading, for Augustine the voice of a child, and for Buechner, a call to laughter.

And for you? The extended hand of a bag woman? The birth of your child?

The tears of the widower? The explosion
of a sunset? The impassioned sermon
that moved all? The dull sermon that
moved none—but you?

It isn't the circumstance that
matters; it is God in the circumstance.
It isn't the words; it is God speaking
them. It wasn't the mud that healed the
eyes of the blind man; it was the finger
of God in the mud. The cradle and the
cross were as common as grass. What
made them holy was the One laid upon
them. The dove and the gull weren't

special. But the One who sent them was.

Amazing, the lengths to which God will go to get our attention.

3

___

READY FOR

HOME

There are many rooms in my Father's house; I would not tell you this if it were not true. I am going there to prepare a place for you.

John 14:2

*H*ad you been on the British Coast in 1845 you might have seen two ships boarded by 138 of England's finest sailors setting sail for the Arctic. Their task? To chart the Northwest Passage around the Canadian Arctic to the Pacific Ocean.

The captain, Sir John Franklin, hoped this effort would be the turning point in Arctic exploration. History shows that it was. Not because of its success, but because of its failure. The ships never returned. Every crew member perished. And those who followed in the expedition's path to the pole learned this lesson: Prepare for the journey.

Apparently Franklin didn't. Though the voyage was projected to last two or three years, he only carried a twelve-day supply of coal for the auxiliary steam engines. But what he lacked in fuel, he made up for in entertainment. Each ship carried a "1,200 volume library, a hand-organ, china place settings for officers and men, cut-glass wine goblets and sterling silver flatware."[6]

Was the crew planning for an Arctic
expedition or a Caribbean cruise?
Judging from the supplies, one would
have thought the latter. The sailors
carried no special clothing to protect
them against the cold. Only the uniforms of Her Majesty's fleet. Noble and
respectful, but thin and inadequate.

The silver knives, forks, and spoons
were as ornate as those found in the
dining rooms of the Royal Navy officers
clubs: heavy at the handles, intricately

designed. Years later, some of these place settings would be found near a clump of frozen, cannibalized bodies.

The inevitable had occurred. The two ships had sailed ill-prepared into the frigid waters. Ice coated the deck, the spars, and the rigging. The sea froze around the rudder and trapped the ship.

The sailors set out to search for help, wearing their uniforms and carrying their belongings. Inuit Indians reported seeing a group dragging a wooden boat across the ice. For the next twenty years, remains of the expedition were found all over the frozen sea. The boat, or a similar one, was later discovered containing the bodies of thirty-five men. Other Indians discovered a tent on the ice and in it, thirty bodies.

Franklin died on the boat. Search parties would later find a piece of the backgammon board Lady Jane Franklin had given her husband as a farewell present.

Many miles from the vessel, the skeleton of a frozen officer was discovered, still wearing trousers and jacket of "fine blue cloth . . . edged with silk braid, with sleeves slashed and bearing five buttons each. Over his uniform the dead man had worn a blue greatcoat, with a black silk neckerchief."[7]

Strange how men could embark on such a journey ill-prepared, more equipped for afternoon tea than for the open sea.

Stranger still how we do the same. Don't Franklin's men remind you of us? We sometimes act as if the Christian life is a retirement cruise. We have little fuel but lots of entertainment. We are more concerned with looking snappy than with being prepared. We give more thought to table settings than to surviving the journey. We give little thought to the destination, but we make sure there's plenty of silver to go around.

And so when the freeze comes, we step out on the ice with forks, games, and skimpy clothing and pass our final days walking against the wind, often blaming God for getting us into this mess.

But God is not to blame. If we sail unprepared it's in spite of—not because of—God. He left detailed instructions about this voyage. His Word is our map; the Holy Spirit is our compass.

He outlined the route and described the landmarks we should seek.

He even told us what to pack for the trip: love, joy, peace, patience, kindness, goodness, faithfulness, gentleness, self-control (see Gal. 5:22–23).

And most remarkably, he's gone before us and goes with us. He's both a pioneer and a co-traveler! And when we grow weary, all we need to do is listen to his voice. He's got special promises to keep us on the journey.

Here is one of the best.

"There are many rooms in my Father's house."

What a tender phrase. A house implies rest, safety, warmth, a table, a bed, a place to be at home. But this isn't just any house. It is our Father's house.

All of us know what it is like to be in a house that is not our own. Perhaps you've spent time in a dorm room or army barrack. Maybe you've slept in your share of hotels or bunked in a few hostels. They have beds. They have tables. They may have food and they may be warm, but they are a far cry from being "your father's house."

Your father's house is where your father is.

Perhaps you can remember the voice of your father? Coming home from work filling the hallways? Sounding through the rooms? Some of you can.

And for many, the memory is fond.

Others of you don't have that memory, but you will. "If my father and mother leave me, the LORD will take me in" (Ps. 27:10).

Your Father is preparing a place for you. A place with *many* rooms. An ample place. A place with space for you. There is a special room for you. You will be welcome.

We don't always feel welcome here on earth. We wonder if there is a place here for us. People can make us feel unwanted. Tragedy leaves us feeling like intruders. Strangers. Interlopers in a land not ours. We don't always feel welcome here.

We shouldn't. This isn't our home. To feel unwelcome is no tragedy. Indeed, it is healthy. We are not home here. This language we speak, it's not ours. This body we wear, it isn't us. And the world we live in, this isn't home.

Ours isn't finished yet.

But when it is, our brother will

come and take us home. "I would not
tell you this if it were not true. . . . I will
come back," he said before he left, "and
take you to be with me so that you may
be where I am" (John 14:2–3).

That first sentence is a curious one.
*"I would not tell you this if it were not
true."* Why did he say that? Did he see
doubt in the heart of the disciples? Did
he read confusion on their faces? I don't
know what he saw in their eyes. But I
know what he sees in ours.

He sees what the airline attendant

sees when she gives her preflight
warnings.

He sees what physicians often see
when they tell patients to stop smoking.

He sees what ministers see when
they tell a Sunday morning audience
that each one of them could die today.

"Yeah, sure. But probably not."

We don't say the words. But we think
them. Sure, this plane could crash, but
then again it probably won't. *So rather
than listen I'll read my magazine. Sure I
could die of cancer, but then again, maybe*

*I won't. So rather than stop smoking today
I'll wait awhile. Sure I could die today,
but then again . . .*

General William Nelson was a
Union general in the Civil War. Though
he faced death every day, he never
prepared for his own. Who knows what
he was thinking as he rode into battle
after battle? Maybe he was too busy
staying alive to prepare for death.

All that changed, however, one day
as he was relaxing in a house with his
men. A brawl broke out, and he was

shot in the chest. Knowing he was dying, he had only one request: "Send for a clergyman."

What had happened? Why the urgency? Did the general suddenly learn something about God that he had never known? No. But he did learn something about himself. He realized death was near. Suddenly only one thing mattered.[8]

Why hadn't it mattered before? Couldn't he have said yes to God the week before or that very morning?

Absolutely. Why didn't he? Why was
the salvation of his soul so urgent after
the shot and so optional before it? Why
had he postponed his decision to accept
Christ until his deathbed?

Because he assumed he had time.

A dangerous assumption. "Teach us
how short our lives really are," prayed
Moses, "so that we may be wise"
(Ps. 90:12).

What fear strikes a man when the
end is near and he's not prepared.

What fear must have struck the

crew of Sir John Franklin when they became stuck in the ice. What anxiety to search for food and find silver, to dig in the closets for coats and find uniforms, to explore the ship for picks and axes and find backgammon games and novels.

Don't you know they would have swapped it all in a heartbeat for what they needed to get home safely?

By the way, what supplies are you taking? Are you carrying your share of silver and games? Don't be fooled; they may matter here, but they matter not when you reach your Father's house. What matters is if you are known by the Father.

It's not what you have; it's who you know. Be prepared. You don't want to be left out in the cold.

4

IF ONLY

YOU KNEW

I have good plans for you, not plans to hurt you. I will give you hope and a good future.

Jeremiah 29:11

W hat I intended as good was interpreted as bad . . . by a humming-bird.

Dozens of the little fellows linger around our house. It's a cordial relationship. We provide the nectar, and they provide the amusement.

Yesterday one of them got into trouble. He flew into the garage and got lost. Though the door was open for him to exit, he didn't see it. He insisted, instead, on bashing his head against a closed window. He was determined to get out, but his determination would not break the glass.

Soon our whole family was in the garage, empathizing with his confusion. "Help him out, Daddy," came the chorus from my kids.

So I tried. I raised the window, hoping he'd fly out—he didn't. He rode the frame as it rose. I nudged him with a broom handle, hoping he'd fly through the open window below. He didn't. I bumped him harder. He wouldn't budge.

Finally, after several firm pokes he made a move . . . the wrong way. Instead of flying forward, he fluttered backward inside the two window panes. Now he was trapped.

What a pitiful sight. A little bird bouncing inside the glass. I had no choice. I stuck my fingers in the opening, grabbed a few feathers, and jerked him out. I'm sure he didn't appreciate the yank, but at least he was free. And when he got back to his nest, did he ever have a story to tell.

I had a horrible day, Martha. I got stuck in this huge room with a fake exit. They made it look like a hole, but it wasn't. Then they tried to crush me with this moving ledge. But it stopped just before it reached the top. The big, ugly one came after me with a stick. Just when he was about to spear me I made a move for it. I dodged him but fell into their trap—a narrow room with invisible walls. How cruel. I could see them pointing at me. I'm sure

*they were hungry. Then the ugly one
came after me again, this time with
his fingers. He was going for my
neck. I outfoxed him, though. Just
when he pulled me out, I kicked
loose and put it in turbocharge and
escaped. It's a good thing I did or
they would have had humming-
burgers for dinner.*

I was being kind. The bird thought
I was cruel. If only the little bird had
known that I had come to help. If only

the little fellow had known that I was on his side. If only he had understood that the moving ledge and stick were for his protection.

If only he knew . . .

Now, I may be overdoing it with the hummingbird, but I'm not overdoing it with the point. Daily, God's extended aid is misinterpreted as intended hurt. We complain of closed windows, not noticing the huge open doors. We panic as the ledge rises, oblivious to the exit below. We dodge the stick that guides and avoid the fingers that liberate.

"If only you knew . . ." were my words to the bird.

"If only you knew . . ." are God's words to us.

No lectures. No speeches. No homilies on how far he has come to help. No finger-pointing at our past. None of that. Just an appeal. An appeal for trust. "If only you knew . . ."

"If only you knew that I came to help and not condemn. If only you knew that tomorrow will be better than today.

If only you knew the gift I have brought:
eternal life. If only you knew I want you
safely home."

If only you knew.

What wistful words to come from
the lips of God. How kind that he would
let us hear them. How crucial that we
pause to hear them. If only we knew to
trust. Trust that God is in our corner.
Trust that God wants what is best. Trust
that he really means it when he says,
"I have good plans for you, not plans to
hurt you. I will give you hope and a

good future" (Jer. 29:11).

If only we could learn to trust him.

But how hard it is. We quiver like the bird on the ledge, ducking the hand that comes to help. We forget that he is the pilot and we are his passenger.

We accuse, falsely. We reject, naively.

If only we knew.

When he washed the disciples' feet, he was washing ours; when he calmed their storms, he was calming yours; when he forgave Peter, he was forgiving all the penitent. If only we knew.

He still sends pigeons to convince the lost and music to inspire the dance.

He still makes our storms his path, our graves his proof, and our souls his passion. He hasn't changed.

He trims branches so we can bear fruit; he calls the sheep that we might be safe; he hears the prayers of crooks so we might go home.

His thunder is still gentle. And his gentleness still thunders.

If only you knew "the free gift of

God and who it is that is asking you . . ."

The gift and the Giver. If you know them, you know all you need.

Notes

1. Francis Thompson, *Poetical Works of Francis Thompson* (New York: Oxford University Press, 1969), 89–94.

2. Ibid.

3. Fred Craddock, *Overhearing the Gospel* (Nashville: Abingdon, 1978), 105–8.

4. Ibid.

5. Frederick Buechner, *The Alphabet of Grace* (New York: HarperCollins, 1970), 43–44.

6. Annie Dillard, *Teaching a Stone to Talk* (New York: HarperCollins, 1988), 43.

7. Ibid.

8. Gary Thomas, "Wise Christians Clip Obituaries," *Christianity Today*, 3 October 1994, 24–27.

Minibooks from Word

Angels Billy Graham

The Applause of Heaven Max Lucado

The Be-Happy Attitudes Robert Schuller

The Finishing Touch Charles Swindoll

A Gentle Thunder Max Lucado

The Gift of Encouraging Words
Florence Littauer

He Still Moves Stones Max Lucado

I'm So Glad You Told Me Barbara Johnson

In the Eye of the Storm Max Lucado

Laugh Again Charles Swindoll

Let's Make a Christmas Memory
Gloria Gaither and Shirley Dobson

Let's Make a Summer Memory
Gloria Gaither and Shirley Dobson

Mama, Get the Hammer! Barbara Johnson

Motherhood Barbara Johnson

On Raising Children
Mary Hollingsworth, compiler

Pack Up Your Gloomees in a Great Big Box
Barbara Johnson

Parenting Isn't for Cowards James Dobson

Peace with God Billy Graham

Silver Boxes Florence Littauer

Splashes of Joy in the Cesspools of Life
Barbara Johnson